W9-AKY-091

DATE DUE

THE MAGIC BAT

Story by Geoffrey Griffin
Illustrations by Don Weller

RSVP
**RAINTREE
STECK-VAUGHN**
PUBLISHERS
The Steck-Vaughn Company

Austin, Texas

To Mrs. Patricia Sabin and my fifth grade class, to my mom and dad,
and to my best friend, Garret Harvey. — G.R.G.

To my goddaughter, Elizabeth. — D.W.

Printed in Mexico.

1 2 3 4 5 6 7 8 9 0 RRD 99 98 97 96 95 94

Library of Congress Cataloging-in-Publication Data

Griffin, Geoffrey, 1982-
     The magic bat / story by Geoffrey Griffin; illustrations
by Don Weller.
        p.   cm. — (Publish-a-book)
     Summary: Geoff is a good baseball player, except that
he always strikes out — until he gets a new "magic" bat.
     ISBN 0-8114-7270-1
     1. Children's writings, American.   [1. Baseball —
Fiction.   2. Children's writings.]   I. Weller, Don, ill.
II. Title.   III. Series.
PZ7.G88135Mag   1995
[Fic] — dc20
                                                94-40434
                                                CIP   AC

My name is Geoff. I want to tell you about my wish and how it came true.

One of my favorite things is to play baseball. A few years ago, I was playing on a team named the Cougars. I was almost the best player on my team. When I pitched, I could get the ball over the plate almost every time. I could also run as fast as the wind and catch any ball that was coming my way.

There was only one thing keeping me from being the Most Valuable Player on my team. I couldn't hit a lick at the plate. My batting was so bad the coach often said, "You can't hit the broad side of a barn."

Every time I was up to bat, the same thing happened. I concentrated as hard as I could on watching the ball. I would swing as hard and as well as I could possibly swing. Then I would hear the umpire yell, "Strike one!" I would bear down and tell myself to focus as I waited for the next pitch. "Strike two!" was most often the result. I would tell myself, "One more chance. I just have to hit it." I'd swing — "Strike three!" I was out again. Oh, how I wished for a magic bat!

I could field, I could run, but I could not bat. The crowd seemed to make it worse. In fact, every time I got up to bat, everyone on the other team would yell, "Easy out!" The parents on my own team would even start praying. What a nightmare it was! Swing, miss — swing, miss — swing, miss.

As I sat on the bench in the dugout and my turn at the plate drew near, the coach would often hear me wish for a magic bat. He would say, "Son, there is no such thing as a magic bat. What you need is to develop confidence in yourself, not magic. You are a good player. You can hit that ball."

My team struggled in second place. I knew if I could have a magic bat, our team could climb into first place, despite what the coach told me.

9

One Friday night, mid-season, my mom called me in to get ready for the game. On the way to the park, she explained that she had to work in the concession stand that night. I was to meet her there immediately after the game.

We were playing the Athletics that night. They were right behind us in third place. It was a close game with our team behind by two runs. It was my turn to bat. The pressure was really on. My teammates, the coach, the crowd — everyone was screaming at me to hit the ball. I stood there and I tried. I tried as hard as I could, but the results were the same. Three strikes. I was out again. Our team ended up losing that game. I felt more strongly than ever that I had let my team down. Long after the team had left, I sat in the dugout wishing again for a magic bat.

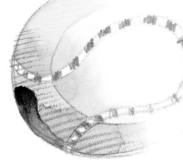

I finally went over to the concession stand to meet my mother. She was still cleaning up, so I laid down my bat and mitt and went inside to help her. After we finished, I went outside to get my things. My mitt was there, but my bat was gone. I panicked! I looked everywhere. It was gone. Someone had stolen it! When I told my mom, she was mad and gave me a speech about being responsible for my things. After a while she was okay, and we went home.

On Saturday morning, my dad took me shopping to get a new bat. We went to three stores before I saw it. It wasn't with the other bats. It was in a corner all by itself. As soon as I saw it, I knew it was special, even though I could tell it had been used before. As I examined the bat, my excitement grew.
I had found it! The perfect bat!
The magic bat!

15

My dad took me as he always did on Saturday to the batting cage. This time I was ready. I had my magic bat. Bam! Bam! Bam! I was hot! This was exactly what I had wished for since T-ball. My wish had finally come true. I could hardly wait for the next game.

Our next game was Thursday night. I practiced my batting for the next four days. My new magic bat was still working like a charm. For the first time in my life I could hit. Fast balls, slow balls, curve balls — it didn't matter. I could hit them all.

17

That Thursday was the longest day of my life. I thought school would never end. Finally, school was over. I was home and dressed for the game at 4:00 P.M. It didn't matter to me at all that the game didn't start until 6:30. I passed the time by practicing my swing in front of the mirror. Two hours later, it was time to go.

When we arrived at the park, I proudly showed off my new bat. The coach told me again that there was no such thing as a magic bat, but I knew better.

Our team was up to bat first, and I was the fourth batter. When I walked to the plate holding my new bat, I knew I couldn't miss. The pitcher and the catcher smiled at each other when they saw me get near the plate.

I could see in their faces that they thought this was going to be an easy out just as before.

The pitcher wound up and threw the ball. Wham! I smacked it right over the fence. My first home run!

The crowd, the coach, and the team went crazy. No one could believe that I hit that ball. What a great feeling!

I was up three more times during that game. I didn't hit another home run, but I got a double and two triples. This magic bat was fabulous!

We had two more games remaining in the season. We still could end up in first place. The next game was the following Thursday night.

As unbelievable as it seems, I smacked two more home runs. Yippee! My team loved me and I was happy. I now had the chance to reach my goal as a Most Valuable Player.

The final game of the season was on Saturday afternoon. If we won, we would be in first place. My chances of receiving the Most Valuable Player award would also improve with a league title. Saturday was going to be the best day of my life.

When I woke up on Saturday morning, it was cloudy and it looked like rain. I just knew the weather could not hold off until afternoon. I felt so disappointed. Just then the phone rang. It was the coach. He said that they had moved up the time of the game, and to come right over to the park.

I was ready in a rush and jumped into the car. I was feeling a little nervous, but mostly I was excited. We pulled into the parking lot. I jumped out of the car, and then I realized that in my excitement I had forgotten my bat, my magic bat. I was so scared. I begged my dad to go home and get my bat, but there was not enough time. I felt sick and I wanted to cry! How could I possibly have forgotten the bat!

The game started. I told the coach I couldn't bat without my magic bat. "That's ridiculous," he said. "You are one of my best players. Use another bat." It was my turn. I picked up one of the bats and slowly walked toward the plate. My knees were shaking so badly I didn't think I would make it. The pitcher wound up and threw the ball. I could see the ball coming toward me. A perfect pitch right over the heart of the plate. I swung. Whack! The ball seemed to explode off the bat and went soaring through the air, right over the fence. A home run! Yes!

We won the game that day. The victory carried our team to first place and a league title. I also received the trophy for the Most Valuable Player. That day was for sure the best day of my life.

When we got home that afternoon, I went to my room to change. Lying on my bed was the magic bat. I looked at the bat and I knew my coach had been right. It wasn't the bat that made me a great hitter. It was **me**!

Geoffrey Griffin, author of **The Magic Bat**, was born on September 30, 1982, in Grosse Pointe, Michigan. He moved to Fort Worth, Texas, in 1988. Geoffrey is an only child and lives with his mom and dad, Karen and Richard.

Geoffrey enjoys playing many sports. He especially likes roller blading, baseball, and playing golf with his dad. He also enjoys skiing during the winter.

As a fifth-grade student at St. Andrew's Catholic School, Geoffrey was sponsored in the 1994 Publish-a-Book Contest by his teacher, Mrs. Patricia Sabin. His story is based on a blend of real-life experiences and imagination. Geoffrey's own bat was stolen, and he had to find a new one to replace it.

After high school, Geoffrey plans to go to college. He would like to get a degree in criminal justice. He knows he will continue to write because it is something that he enjoys doing.

The twenty honorable-mention winners in the **1994 Raintree/Steck-Vaughn Publish-a-Book Contest** were Dennis J. Lee, Bowen School, Newton, Massachusetts; Jessica Stephen, Harborside School, Milford, Connecticut; Cassandra Gaddo, Southview Elementary School, Waconia, Minnesota; Emily Hinson, Robert E. Lee Elementary School, East Wenatchee, Washington; Jessie Manning, Rice Lake Elementary School, Maple Grove, Minnesota; Neil Finfrock, Brimfield Elementary, Kent, Ohio; Andrew Campbell, St. Eugene's School, Santa Rosa, California; Tiffany McDermott, St. Rose of Lima School, Freehold, New Jersey; Laura Dorval, Riverside Middle School, Chattaroy, Washington; Alison Taylor, Fisher Elementary School, Oklahoma City, Oklahoma; Kendra Hennig, East Farms School, Farmington, Connecticut; Lisa Walters, Northeast Elementary School, Kearney, Nebraska; Hunter Stitik, Forest Oak Elementary School, Newark, Delaware; Jamie Pucka, Rensselaer Central Middle School, Rensselaer, Indiana; April Wagner, Monte Vista Middle School, San Jacinto, California; Elizabeth Neale, Clifton Springs Elementary School, Clifton Springs, New York; Rachel Kuehn, Roseville Public Library, Roseville, California; Carolyn Blessing, John Diemer School, Overland Park, Kansas; Kelsey Condra, Grace Academy of Dallas, Dallas, Texas; Michael Gildener-Leapman, Charles E. Smith Jewish Day School, Rockville, Maryland.

Don Weller, a graphic designer and illustrator, is the founder of the Weller Institute for the Cure of Design. He has won many awards for his work, including a Lifetime Achievement Award from the Los Angeles Society of Illustrators. He has published three books. *Park City* and *Seashells and Sunsets* were both acclaimed by the American Institute of Graphic Arts. His most recent book is *The Cutting Horse*, which he wrote and photographed. He has illustrated numerous books, including *Phantom of the Opera* and *Professor Fergus Fahrenheit and His Wonderful Weather Machine*. He lives in Park City, Utah.